£4.99

12

CONTENTS

Written by Laurence Anthony.
Design by Sue Bartram.

Published by
Grandreams Limited
Jadwin House, 205-211 Kentish Town Road,
London, NW5 2JU.

Printed in Italy.

THE STORY OF A SEASON... Part 1

Above: Aerial action in the win against Swindon

In 1992-93 Manchester United enjoyed their finest season in years.

For the first time since 1966-67, the Red Devils won the title - as the first-ever Champions of the Premier League - and they did it in true style. The final table of the season saw United finishing ten points ahead of closest rivals Aston Villa, and the relief was felt all around Old Trafford. United had done it...there was nothing else to prove. Except, of course, whether they could do it all over again in 1993-94.

The new Champs hit the headlines again in the summer when they won the race for the signature of Nottingham Forest star midfielder Roy Keane. At £3.75 million, the Republic of Ireland international became the then-most expensive player ever to move between two British clubs.

Keane, looking a bit rusty and slightly unfit, made his first team debut for United in the 1993 Charity Shield match, against FA Cup holders, ARSENAL, at Wembley.

Mark Hughes opened

Right: United's Paul Ince in a tussle for the ball with Robert Lee of Newcastle

the scoring after just eight minutes when he hit a spectacular scissors-kick into David Seaman's net. The opening came from a neat move involving Denis Irwin and Eric Cantona. The Gunners fought back and, five minutes before half-time, Ian Wright whacked a shot past Peter Schmeichel from almost 20 yards out.

There were no more goals in the second half and the game went to a penalty shoot-out. The matter was resolved when United's 'keeper Peter Schmeichel faced up to his opposite number, David Seaman, at the sudden-death stage. The Arsenal 'keeper struck the ball, the United 'keeper saved it. United had won 5-4 on penalties.

Manchester United's Premiership campaign got under way on Sunday 15 August, away to NORWICH CITY. In the previous season, the Canaries had given both United and Villa a good run for their money and had finished in a healthy third place. In this game, things seemed evenly balanced between the two sides for the first 25 minutes. Then Ryan Giggs struck United's first goal of the campaign after latching on to a Mark Hughes effort which had rebounded off the crossbar.

Lee Sharpe is challenged by Arsenal's Eddie McGoldrick

Nine minutes into the second half Bryan Robson opened his account when he finished off a move by Paul Ince and Mark Hughes. United old-boy Mark Robins brought out the best in Peter Schmeichel with a lethal-looking effort. But the save was equal to it and United held on to their lead and their first three points of the season.

On the following Wednesday evening, SHEFFIELD UNITED were Old Trafford's first visitors of the season. New-boy Roy Keane proved an instant hit on his home debut when he smashed home the first goal

Mark Hughes cuts his way through the Spurs' defence

Ryan Giggs gets ahead of Wednesday's Mark Bright

of the game, after 16 minutes. And he was a real hero 27 minutes later when he struck a second in a move begun by an Andrei Kanchelskis free-kick. With five minutes left, Mark Hughes got his first League goal of the season, to round off the scoreline at 3-0. United dropped their first points of the campaign in a 1-1 draw with Premiership new-boys NEWCASTLE UNITED at Old Trafford on 21 August. Ryan Giggs scored for the home side in the first half. Andy Cole replied for the visitors in the 80th minute.

United were in action again just two days later away to ASTON VILLA. It was a brilliant game, worthy of two of the top teams in the country. Lee Sharpe scored first on 18 minutes, after rounding Earl Barrett. Dalian Atkinson equalised for Villa, after making a stunning 40 yard run, on the stroke of half-time. But it was to be Lee Sharpe's match - he struck United's winner after a run of his own with 15 minutes left to play.

United next travelled to the south coast to take on SOUTHAMPTON at The Dell. Again the Red Devils were in Championship-form. Three first-half goals - from Lee Sharpe, Eric Cantona and Denis Irwin - were enough to seal the points. Neil Maddison replied for the Saints.

United collected another three points from the visit of WEST HAM UNITED on the first day of September. That man Sharpe struck his fourth goal of the campaign when he headed home Andrei Kanchelskis' deadly accurate cross in the 6th minute. Eric Cantona widened the gap when he converted a penalty just before half-time, after Ludek Miklosko had upended Roy Keane in the box. Man-of-the-Match Sharpe was involved in the third goal, supplying Steve Bruce with a superb cross, to head home in the 88th

MATCH-FAX...AUGUST-SEPTEMBER 1993

FA Charity Shield			
7.8.93	Wembley Stadium (United won 5-4 on penalties)	Att: 66,519	ARSENAL 1, UNITED 1
Premiership			
15.8.93	Carrow Road	Att: 19,705	NORWICH 0, UNITED 2
18.8.93	Old Trafford	Att: 41,949	UNITED 3, SHEFFIELD UTD 0
21.8.93	Old Trafford	Att: 41,829	UNITED 1, NEWCASTLE UTD 1
23.8.93	Villa Park	Att: 39,624	ASTON VILLA 1, UNITED 2
28.8.93	The Dell	Att: 16,189	SOUTHAMPTON 1, UNITED 3
1.9.93	Old Trafford	Att: 44,613	UNITED 3, WEST HAM 0
11.9.93	Stamford Bridge	Att: 37,064	CHELSEA 1, UNITED 0
19.9.93	Old Trafford	Att: 44,009	UNITED 1, ARSENAL 0
25.9.93	Old Trafford	Att: 44,583	UNITED 4, SWINDON 2
Coca-Cola Cup Second Round, First Leg			
22.9.93	Victoria Ground	Att: 23,327	STOKE CITY 2, UNITED 1

minute.

England's World Cup action held up the Premiership's progress for ten days and when normal service resumed, United found themselves on the wrong end of a scoreline for the first time in six months. Glenn Hoddle's CHELSEA, having gained an early lead through Gavin Peacock, played superbly to keep out United's onslaught and hold on to the points.

Four days later, United travelled to Budapest in Hungary to make their return to the European Cup competition against HONVED (see 'Into Europe - Out Of Europe' page 14)

19 September saw United back at Old Trafford and playing ARSENAL in the Premiership. In the 36th minute Paul Ince took a free-kick, gently rolling the ball into the path of Eric Cantona. The French ace hit a perfect shot from 25 yards which beat David Seaman. It was the only goal of the game.

The Red Devils received a shock in the Coca-Cola Cup Second Round, First Leg on 22 September, when they lost 2-1 away to STOKE CITY. Mark Stein did the damage for the Potters, scoring both goals either side of Dion Dublin's reply for United.

United's last game in September was at home to newly-promoted SWINDON TOWN. The Wiltshire club had had a poor start to life in the Premiership - they were lying at the foot of the table, without a win, and United did nothing to improve their position. In fact, they worsened it with a 4-2 victory. United's goals came from Andrei Kanchelskis, Eric Cantona and Mark Hughes who scored twice.

As the month ended Manchester United were sitting on top of the table,

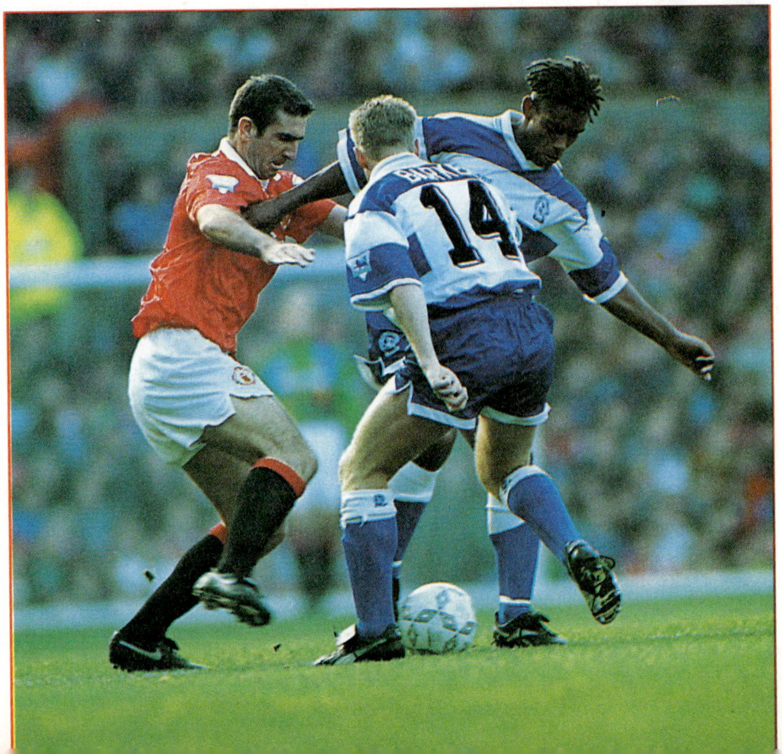

'Let me in!' says Eric Cantona, in the game against QPR

Ooh La, it's Cantona, tantalising the Ipswich defence

with 22 points - three ahead of Arsenal.

It was destination Hillsborough, home of SHEFFIELD WEDNESDAY, for United's first game in October. Wednesday went ahead, through Chris Bart-Williams on 47 minutes - but three minutes later, United were back on level terms when Mark Hughes hit home a Lee Sharpe cross.

Hughes was on target again 16 minutes later, finishing off a brilliant move created by Eric Cantona. Ryan Giggs made it 3-1 when he got the better of Chris Woods to slot the ball into the gaping goal. Still Wednesday were not done, they came back and scored another, through Mark Bright with four minutes left.

Wednesday 6 October saw the Coca-Cola Cup Second Leg game against STOKE. 41,548 fans turned out to see if United could rescue the situation. In the event, Bryan Robson, the proudest player in the Premiership, inspired United to a great performance. But the goals didn't come until the second half - from Lee Sharpe and Brian McClair. United went through 3-2 on aggregate.

World Cup business again interrupted the Premier programme, with no less than nine United players on international duty, and the Red Devils did not play again until 16 October, when TOTTENHAM HOTSPUR came to Old Trafford. All the goals came late in the game. Roy Keane opened the scoring in the 65th minute, and Lee Sharpe added another two minutes later. Darren Caskey replied for Spurs.

EVERTON were United's opposition on 23 October at Goodison Park. There was only one goal in the game - but what a goal it was! A great volley by Lee Sharpe who had latched onto a poor clearance out of the Everton defence.

LEICESTER CITY came to Old Trafford in the Coca-Cola Cup Third Round on 27 October - and they were thrashed. Goals from Steve Bruce (2), Brian McClair, Lee Sharpe and Mark Hughes underlined United's superiority. The final score was 5-1. Steve Bruce had cause to celebrate as his opening goal was the 100th in his career, a remarkable record for a defender.

QUEENS PARK

MATCH-FAX...OCTOBER 1993

Premiership			
2.10.93	Hillsborough	Att: 34,548	SHEFFIELD WED 2, UNITED 3
16.10.93	Old Trafford	Att: 44,655	UNITED 2, SPURS 1
23.10.93	Goodison Park	Att: 35,430	EVERTON 0, UNITED 1
30.10.93	Old Trafford	Att: 44,633	UNITED 2, QPR 1
Coca-Cola Cup Second Round, Second Leg			
6.10.93	Old Trafford	Att: 41,387	UNITED 2, STOKE CITY 0
	(United won 3-2 on aggregate)		
Coca-Cola Cup Third Round			
27.10.93	Old Trafford	Att: 41,344	UNITED 5, LEICESTER CITY 1

RANGERS visited Old Trafford on the final Saturday in October. After Bradley Allen had given Rangers an early lead, Eric Cantona and Mark Hughes became the stars of the show. Cantona put in an incredible run from at least half way. He dummied two defenders, then shot in off the post for the equaliser. Mark Hughes scored the winner after a Lee Sharpe corner kick had been expertly flicked on by Roy Keane.

Lee Sharpe in action against Ipswich

Manchester United's remarkable run of form saw them comfortably ahead of the Premier pack at the end of October. They had 34 points. Closest rivals Norwich, Arsenal and Blackburn lagged a long way behind with 23 points each.

Having been unceremoniously dumped out of the European Cup competition by Galatasaray, United resumed their Premiership challenge with a 3-2 away win in the local derby with MANCHESTER CITY.

It was City who made the early running with two first-half goals from Niall Quinn. United knew they had to pull themselves together if they were going to salvage anything from the game. And that's precisely what they did.

On 52 minutes Eric Cantona took advantage of a poor back pass and scored from the edge of the area. In the 77th minute Ryan Giggs set up the equaliser with a brilliant run and cross which Cantona tapped home. The winner came with just four minutes left, when Roy Keane headed in a Denis Irwin cross. The comeback was complete.

Eric Cantona and Lee Sharpe celebrate the Frenchman's goal against Coventry

The Premiership programme was again interrupted by World Cup action (England were eliminated on 18 November) and so United's next game took place on 20 November at Old Trafford where the visitors were WIMBLEDON. Second-half goals from Gary Pallister, Mark Hughes and Andrei Kanchelskis gave United an emphatic victory. John Fashanu replied for the Dons.

Four days later, United entertained IPSWICH TOWN at Old Trafford in what turned out to be a game dominated by the two defences. Neither could be broken down and the match ended in a 0-0 stalemate. It was the first time United had failed to find the net at home all season.

United's flying winger Andrei Kanchelskis - on the ball against Norwich

The following Saturday saw United's challenge get back on course with a 1-0 away victory over COVENTRY CITY. The goal came on the hour and was scored by Eric Cantona. But United had to battle towards the end of the game to keep out Coventry's onslaught.

On 30 November United met EVERTON in the Fourth Round of the Coca-Cola Cup at Goodison Park. By half-time, they were 2-0 ahead, through Mark Hughes and Ryan Giggs. Everton's Tony Cottee came closest to a goal when he reluctantly took a penalty kick. Peter Schmeichel pulled off a brilliant save and the scoreline remained unchanged.

At the end of November, United were a comfortable 14 points ahead of nearest rivals Leeds in the Premiership.

The first Saturday in December saw United at home to NORWICH CITY, who were putting in a strong challenge on the Premiership's leading pack.

It proved to be a great game. After half an hour both sides scored within the space of a minute - Ryan Giggs for United, Chris Sutton for the Canaries. Ten minutes later, Brian McClair shot United into the lead from inside the area following an Eric Cantona flick-on and a Ryan Giggs pass.

Unfortunately for United, Gary Pallister gave away a penalty just after half-time - and Ruel Fox equalised from the spot. The points were shared.

On 7 December, United travelled to Bramall Lane to play struggling SHEFFIELD UNITED - and they went home again with all three points safely in the bag.

Mark Hughes opened the scoring after 13 minutes with a shot from the edge of the area. Lee Sharpe extended the lead on 27 minutes after beating the offside trap. And, on the hour, Eric Cantona finished off a 50-yard run with a goal from a magnificent angled

Mark Hughes wards off a Sheffield United challenge

shot.

The following Saturday, United went to the north-east to take on Kevin Keegan's NEWCASTLE UNITED. It was an exciting game, with the scoreline at 0-0 after 45 minutes. Then, with half an hour to go, Andrei Kanchelskis fed Paul Ince

MATCHFAX...NOVEMBER 1993

Premiership			
7.11.93	Maine Road	Att: 35,155	MANCHESTER CITY 2, UNITED 3
20.11.93	Old Trafford	Att: 44,748	UNITED 3, WIMBLEDON 1
24.11.93	Old Trafford	Att: 43,300	UNITED 0, IPSWICH TOWN 0
27.11.93	Highfield Road	Att: 17,000	COVENTRY CITY 0, UNITED 1
Coca-Cola Cup Fourth Round			
30.11.93	Goodison Park	Att: 34,050	EVERTON 0, UNITED 2

INTO EUROPE - OUT OF EUROPE

United's European adventure in the 1993-94 European Cup competition lasted just two rounds. After eliminating Hungarian side HONVED, they fell to Turkish Champions GALATASARAY. Here are the results...

First Round

15.9.93 Jozef Bozsic Stadium	Att: 9,000	HONVED 2, UNITED 3
29.9.93 Old Trafford	Att: 35,781	UNITED 2, HONVED 1
		(United won 5-3 on aggregate)

Second Round

20.10.93 Old Trafford	Att: 39,396	UNITED 3, GALATASARAY 3,
3.11.93 Ali Sami Yen	Att: -	GALATASARAY 0, UNITED 0
		(Galatasaray won on away-goals rule)

Action from United v Blackburn

with a well-placed pass from which he scored with a left-foot drive.

The Magpies' danger-man Andy Cole headed the equaliser eleven minutes later - and that's how the score remained.

On Sunday 19 December, United entertained ASTON VILLA at Old Trafford. With just minutes to go, it looked like being a 1-0 win for United following Eric Cantona's 21st minute goal from a Roy Keane cross.

Then came an exciting finale. In the 89th minute Steve Bruce put Cantona through, and he scored from 12 yards out. In injury time, Paul Ince added to United's total with a well-placed shot from 10 yards. To add to the thrills, Villa's Neil Cox also scored a goal to make it 3-1 - all of which all goes to show that no-one should ever leave a football

Eric Cantona has just scored against Villa

ground until the final whistle has been blown!

Third-placed BLACKBURN ROVERS came to Old Trafford for the first game after Christmas. Kevin Gallacher turned on a Ryan Giggs-like display on 15 minutes when he bamboozled the United defence to open the scoring. For a long time after that it looked as though United were about to suffer their first home defeat of the campaign. But, with their never-say-die spirit, they battled on until the equaliser came - with just two minutes to go. Paul Ince was the scorer from a goalmouth melee.

United finished off 1993 with a real cracker when they met OLDHAM ATHLETIC at Boundary Park. United were one up after just four minutes when Andrei

Andrei Kanchelskis scores against Oldham

Kanchelskis beat Jon Hallworth after two attempts. Graeme Sharp equalised for the Latics eleven minutes later. Three minutes after that, Eric Cantona blasted the ball home from the penalty spot after Kanchelskis had been upended.

Rick Holden pulled Oldham back into the game on 26 minutes with a magnificent free-kick, taken near the touch line, which beat Peter Schmeichel. Twelve minutes later and United were back in front. This time the goal came from a Steve Bruce header.

In the second half, Ryan Giggs ran riot, scoring twice to round off the scoreline at 5-2 to United.

As 1993 drew to a close, Manchester United were sitting comfortably on top of the Premier League table with 57 points. Following them on 45 points were Kenny Dalglish's Blackburn...

The Story of a Season continues on page 34...

MATCH FAX...DECEMBER 1993

Premiership			
4.12.93	Old Trafford	Att: 44,649	UNITED 2, NORWICH CITY 2
7.12.93	Bramall Lane	Att: 26,744	SHEFFIELD UNITED 0, UNITED 3
11.12.93	St James' Park	Att: 36,388	NEWCASTLE UNITED 1, UNITED 1
19.12.93	Old Trafford	Att: 44,499	UNITED 3, ASTON VILLA 1
26.12.93	Old Trafford	Att: 44,511	UNITED 1, BLACKBURN ROVERS 1
29.12.93	Boundary Park	Att: 16,709	OLDHAM ATHLETIC 2, UNITED 5

THE TEAM THAT ALEX BUILT...

...KEEPING 'EM OUT!

Since he was appointed Manchester United's manager in 1986, Alex Ferguson has honed Old Trafford's pool of players into one of the finest club sides in the world. His current squad is a mix of home-grown talent and shrewd acquisitions in the transfer market...

Oldham Athletic's Craig Fleming reckons that United are dangerous, even when their goalkeeper has the ball! And how right he is, for Peter Schmeichel is one of the very best distributors of the ball in the entire Premiership.

His throwing is so strong and so accurate that Fergie must sometimes feel that he has an extra player out there!

Towering 6'4" above his area, Peter is an imposing presence, enough to put the frighteners into any attacker! He is also a great stopper of seemingly 'unstoppable' shots.

Many soccer pundits reckon he is the finest all-

Les Sealey's in goal

Peter Schmeichel gets down to the ball

round goalkeeper in Europe - others say the world. Few would argue the point.

Peter arrived at Old Trafford from Danish club Brondby in 1991, having been voted Denmark's 'Player of the Year' in the previous season. Since then he has settled in as United's first-choice keeper, and a remarkably consistent one at that. For instance, in the 1992-93 Premiership-winning campaign he conceded only 31 goals in 42 games.

In the summer of 1992, he was a vital member of Denmark's glorious European Championship success.

United's second-string keeper is Les Sealey, currently in his second spell with the club. A tremendous character with plenty to say for himself both on and off the pitch, he invariably wears a huge and happy smile!

Les has become something of a specialist at playing at Wembley. As a replacement for Jim Leighton, he won an FA Cup winners' medal with United in 1990. And in 1994, standing-in for the suspended Peter Schmeichel, he took home a Coca-Cola runners-up medal.

THE TEAM THAT ALEX BUILT...

When the going gets tough...the tough get going! A wounded and bandaged Steve Bruce battles on

...THE DEFENDERS

A settled, mean-spirited defence is essential for any club intending to chase the game's top honours.

And, since Gary Pallister, Steve Bruce, Denis Irwin and Paul Parker started playing together as a unit, United's 'goals against' column has looked extremely healthy and the trophies have started to roll in.

Club captain Steve Bruce - he took over the role from Bryan Robson - has a great understanding with Gary Pallister. Together they form the most devastating central defensive partnership in the Premiership.

Steve, a Geordie, arrived at Old Trafford in December 1987, in a £825,000 transfer deal from Norwich City. Previously he had been with Gillingham.

Not only a fine defender, he also has a penchant for scoring goals of which he has now amassed over 100 in his career.

When Gary Pallister arrived at Old Trafford from Middlesbrough in September 1989, he was then - at £2.3 million - the most expensive player to move between two British clubs.

Many who questioned the figure at the time, now regret their words - because Gary has proven himself worth every penny of that gigantic fee. Since joining United, he has collected a whole hatful of honours.

Gary made his England debut in April 1988 against Hungary and has continued to impress on the international scene.

United's skipper Steve Bruce celebrates a goal!

Mr Pallister deals with Mr Wright!

Right back Paul Parker is a composed, unflappable defender with great pace and a liking for attack.

A Londoner, he began with Thames-siders Fulham in 1980-81. Seven seasons later he moved just a mile or so northwards to Queens Park Rangers. He came to Old Trafford for £1.5 million in the summer of 1990, having impressed everyone with his polished performances for England in the World Cup Finals in Italy.

He is now a vital cog in Alex Ferguson's magical football machine.

Denis Irwin is a world class defender, as he has proved in numerous outings with Jack Charlton's Republic of Ireland side.

His career began with Leeds United, but he failed to shine at Elland Road and was given a free transfer. Joe Royle, boss of Oldham Athletic, took advantage of the situation and brought him to Boundary Park in 1986.

With Oldham, Denis began to flourish. He developed into a fine full back and was soon catching the eye of the bigger clubs.

It was after two magnificent FA Cup semi-final performances for the Latics against United in 1990, that Alex Ferguson decided to put in a bid for him.

As a result, Denis moved to Old Trafford in a £625,000 transfer deal. He began in the right back berth, but switched to left back with the arrival of Paul Parker...And another piece of Alex Ferguson's jigsaw puzzle slotted into place.

Like Paul Parker, Denis has a talent for going forward. He is the instigator of many a United attack and the occasional scorer of fine goals. He is also something of a free-kick expert.

The world class Denis Irwin

Paul Parker and Steve Bruce put in a double challenge on Blackburn's Alan Shearer

THE TEAM THAT ALEX BUILT...

Roy Keane celebrates another United goal!

When Nottingham Forest were relegated to the First Division in 1992-93, it was inevitable that superstar Roy Keane would move on.

Before he made that move, there was much speculation as to where the Republic of Ireland's midfield ace would go. Blackburn Rovers and Arsenal were among the front runners. But Keane -

Roy Keane eludes a Tottenham tackle

keen to perform in the European Cup - finally chose Manchester United.

The £3.75 million transfer fee was a British record, but boss Alex Ferguson reckoned Roy was well worth it. Indeed, Fergie sees him as a natural successor to United's legendary Bryan Robson.

That's some act to follow - but Roy is as Keane as mustard to do well in the famous red shirt!

Roy made his United debut in the Charity Shield match against Arsenal at Wembley and has since become a great favourite with the Old Trafford fans.

Paul Ince has come on by leaps and bounds since joining United from West Ham for £1.75 million in 1989 - and he was already a formidable talent then!

A player of vision, strength and superb ability, he now enjoys a vital role in United's midfield engine room.

Intense concentration from Paul Ince

Paul captained England against the U.S.A. and Brazil in June 1993 and is now important to Terry Venables' England expectations. He will no doubt play a leading role in the European Championship drama due to unfold in England in 1996.

The versatile Lee Sharpe

Brian McClair on the ball

Bryan Robson, one of the all-time greats of English football, may be nearing the end of his playing career, but he still gives 100% whenever he pulls on a Manchester United shirt.

And that's the way it's been for 'Robbo' ever since he arrived at Old Trafford in 1981. He was bought by then manager Ron Atkinson for £1.5 million from West Brom, the club they had both served so well.

He quickly became club captain, and led United to FA Cup success in 1983, '85 and '90. But the highlight of his club career came in May 1993 when he collected a League Championship medal. No-one deserved it more.

Bryan played 90 times for England and on many occasions was an inspirational captain. If not for the number of injuries he sustained during his full-blooded career, he might well have broken Peter Shilton's record of 125 caps!

Robbo is still closely involved with the England set-up, as right-hand man to coach Terry Venables.

Once a committed striker for United, Brian McClair has now assumed a role that links midfield and attack. And he does it extremely effectively.

Brian was one of Alex Ferguson's initial signings when he took over the reins at Old Trafford. The Scottish striker had been performing brilliantly with Celtic when Fergie snapped him up for £850,000 in July 1987. The outlay was considered well worthwhile when he became the first United player in twenty years to net more than twenty League goals in a season.

Brian was ever-present during United's glorious Premiership-winning campaign of 1992-93.

A couple of seasons ago, it was touch and go

Bryan Robson - United's inspiration for many seasons

whether Lee Sharpe would be able to continue his career as a professional footballer. At the time, he was suffering from viral meningitis and his footballing days were definitely under threat.

Happily, he made a full recovery and returned to full strength. His career is back on course, and no-one is more delighted than Alex Ferguson who first spotted the lad's potential when he was a full back with Torquay United.

Fergie parted with £125,000 of United's money to bring Lee to Old Trafford and he has since proved one of the great bargain buys in recent football history.

Lee is a versatile player, often seen on the left side of midfield, but is equally effective on the left wing. He is also a capable defender when the need arises.

Mark Hughes shows his aggression against the Wimbledon defence

THE TEAM THAT ALEX BUILT...

...THE STRIKE FORCE

There are two types of striker - great scorers of goals, and scorers of great goals.

Mark 'Sparky' Hughes definitely belongs in the second category as some of his spectacular bicycle-kicks and volleys have shown over the seasons.

Mark's assets are plain to see - he is aggressive, powerful, strong and fearless. He is also one of the best headers of a ball in British football and is equally adept at shielding a ball with his back to goal, before laying it off to a better-placed team-mate.

Mark is now in his second spell with United. He started at Old Trafford as an apprentice and turned professional in November 1980. He went on to become one of United's great stars, scoring 37 League goals in 85 appearances between '83 and '85.

He was then snapped up by Terry Venables at

Barcelona, but things didn't work out as well as expected and Sparky was soon loaned out to Bayern Munich in Germany.

Then in 1988, Alex Ferguson pulled off a managerial masterstroke by bringing him back to United where he has continued to shine ever since.

Many people consider Andrei Kanchelskis United's best player. The dashing winger is certainly among the most exciting to watch!

Born in Kirovograd, in the former U.S.S.R., he came to United in March 1991 after being a star turn with Dinamo Kiev and Shakytor Donetsk of the Russian League.

After a trial period, Alex Ferguson was so impressed with Andrei that he offered him a full-time contract and paid Shakytor Donetsk £650,000 for his services.

Andrei made a sensational debut for United against Notts County and he's been a great favourite with the Old Trafford faithful ever since.

Mark Hughes - a great 'shielder' of the ball

Ryan Giggs is the most sensational young player to burst onto the British soccer scene in many a season.

Born in Cardiff in November 1973, he was brought up in Manchester and almost followed his father into Rugby League. But soccer won out in the end and Manchester City first spotted the lad's potential when he was a schoolboy. But it was neighbouring United who took him on as an associated schoolboy in February 1988.

From then on, Ryan, an England schoolboy international, was to progress through the United ranks until he turned professional in December 1990. He made his first-team debut as a sub against Everton at Old Trafford on 2 March 1991.

Since then, young Ryan has gone from strength to strength and is the idol of every schoolboy in the country, a role model they'd all love to emulate.

Blessed with skill, speed, a lethal left foot and

United's Andrei Kanchelskis - one of the fastest forwards in the Premiership

Eric Cantona gets away from Villa's Paul McGrath

Dion Dublin

a touch of genius, Ryan has been compared to the legendary George Best, United's star winger of the late-60s and early-70s.

Just twenty-one this year, he has already collected a hatful of honours and has twice been voted the PFA's 'Young Player of the Year'.

Eric Cantona is a marvellously inventive footballer full of flair and skill. He also has a dark side which often gets his name inscribed in referees' bad books!

Alex Ferguson brought the fabulous Frenchman to Old Trafford in November 1992 when Eric failed to see eye to eye with Howard Wilkinson at Leeds.

After a stormy and controversial career in France, he first arrived in England in January 1992, fully expecting to sign for Trevor Francis' Sheffield Wednesday. In the event, Eric did not kick a ball in a Wednesday shirt.

Instead, he joined Leeds United where despite making just six first-team appearances, plus nine as substitute, he was influential in Leeds' run-in to their 1991-92 title success.

Then, just over six months later, Cantona felt that he was spending a little too much time on the Leeds bench and he was soon on the move again - this time

'Hail, the conquering hero!' Cantona celebrates another goal

to Old Trafford. And this time, he was to help Manchester United to Championship success, thereby becoming the first player to collect title medals with different clubs in successive seasons.

The shrewd Alex Ferguson always has special players in reserve. Among them is super-striker Dion Dublin who arrived at Old Trafford for £1 million from Cambridge United in August 1992. But he had only played in a handful of matches for United when he broke his leg and was out of the game for several months.

Now Dion is striving to regain a first-team place in Alex Ferguson's super-squad.

Ryan Giggs mesmerises the ball

RED DEVILS

Some brilliant United action-shots from our photo gallery...

Andrei Kanchelskis on the move against Swindon

IN ACTION...

Top: Paul Ince gets to the ball ahead of QPR's David Bardsley

Above: Lee Sharpe in action against Wimbledon

Left: Mark Hughes rides a tackle from Charlton's Alan Pardew in the FA Cup 6th Round

Liverpool's Nigel Clough and United's Eric Cantona in arguably the finest match of the season - the 3-3 draw at Anfield

THE STORY OF A SEASON Part 2

LEEDS UNITED, chasing the Premiership leaders, came to Old Trafford on New Year's Day. 44,724 fans turned out to watch a hard fought 0-0 draw, in which neither side was prepared to give at all. Indeed, throughout the entire 90 minutes both teams each managed no more than a couple of shots on goal.

If the Leeds game had been a bit of a disappointment, then United's next match, away to LIVERPOOL, was a veritable feast of excitement and endeavour. For the first 23 minutes United looked every inch the unstoppable Champions as Steve Bruce, Ryan Giggs and Denis Irwin blasted them into a 3-0 lead. Then suddenly, Liverpool were back in the game when a long-range shot from Neil Ruddock beat Peter Schmeichel. And by half-time the gap had narrowed to 3-2 - Nigel Clough had hammered home a stray ball.

United fought to hold on to their now slender lead. But with 11 minutes to go, Neil Ruddock headed Liverpool's equaliser - and the points were shared in what would later be regarded as The Game of the Season.

Sunday 9 January saw Manchester United's entry into the 1994 FA Cup competition with a visit to SHEFFIELD UNITED. Having twice beaten the Blades 3-0 earlier in the season, many considered that this game would be a mere formality for United.

In fact, it was an evenly-matched, if

unfriendly, affair - with Dave Bassett's side holding out well against the favourites. It took a fabulous strike by Mark Hughes, on 63 minutes, to break the deadlock and send United through to the Fourth Round.

On Wednesday 12 January PORTSMOUTH came to Old Trafford for the Coca-Cola Cup Fifth Round clash - and they proceeded to give United a real run for their money. Indeed, Pompey kept pace throughout the game and were well worth their 2-2 draw. United's goals came from Ryan Giggs (29 mins) and Eric Cantona (60 mins).

The following Saturday, United resumed their Premiership challenge with a visit to TOTTENHAM HOTSPUR. Shortly after half-time Mark Hughes met a well-placed Roy Keane cross at the near post and nudged the ball home.

Later, Keane himself also had the ball in the net - but referee Roger Milford ruled Eric Cantona offside and the score remained at 1-0. United had collected three more precious points.

Before United's next game, at home to EVERTON on 22 January, the whole of the footballing world was saddened by the death of Sir Matt Busby, Manchester United's great mentor of the 1940s, '50s and '60s. Sir Matt had led the club to League Championship success in 1956 and 1957. He had then survived the Munich air crash of February 1958 which had virtually destroyed his team of young talents.

After that, he patiently rebuilt his beloved Manchester United team and, in 1968, led them to European Cup glory as the first English club to win that coveted trophy.

Following his retirement from management, Sir Matt had remained involved with the club and was happy and proud to witness United's Premiership triumph of 1992-93. Now he was gone.

Before the match against Everton kicked-off, the one minute silent tribute to United's greatest servant, observed by 44,750 spectators, was a moving and emotional farewell to a good friend.

Sir Matt would have enjoyed the game that followed. It was full of entertainment and flowing football. And United took all three points, thanks to a Ryan Giggs goal headed home on 26 minutes.

Next came the Coca-Cola Cup Fifth Round replay away to PORTSMOUTH. This time, try as they might, Pompey had no answer to United and the Red Devils went through to the semi-finals with a 1-0 victory. Brian McClair was the scorer on 27 minutes after a Ryan Giggs corner had been flicked on by Eric Cantona.

United ended January with another cup clash - this time away to NORWICH CITY in the Fourth Round of the FA Cup. On 18 minutes Ryan Giggs pared open the Canaries' defence with a magnificent run. He then passed to Andrei Kanchelskis who supplied the pass from which Roy Keane opened the scoring.

MATCH FAX...JANUARY 1994

Premiership			
1.1.94	Old Trafford	Att: 44,724	UNITED 0, LEEDS UNITED 0
4.1.94	Anfield	Att: 42,795	LIVERPOOL 3, UNITED 3
15.1.94	White Hart Lane	Att: 31,343	SPURS 0, UNITED 1
22.1.94	Old Trafford	Att: 44,750	UNITED 1, EVERTON 0
FA Cup Third Round			
9.1.94	Bramall Lane	Att: 22,019	SHEFFIELD UNITED 0, UNITED 1
FA Cup Fourth Round			
31.1.94	Carrow Road	Att: 21,070	NORWICH CITY 0, UNITED 2
Coca-Cola Cup Fifth Round			
12.1.94	Old Trafford	Att: 43,794	UNITED 2, PORTSMOUTH 2
Coca-Cola Cup Fifth Round Replay			
26.1.94	Fratton Park	Att: 24,950	PORTSMOUTH 0, UNITED 1

Ryan Giggs about to score a fabulous goal against QPR

Norwich went close a couple of times, but Peter Schmeichel was always on hand to deal with the situation. Then, in the 73rd minute, Eric Cantona sealed the match with an opportunists' strike when he seized on a poor back pass by the City defence.

And so things were looking good for United at the end of January. They were top of the table and were still in both Cup competitions. The 'treble' was firmly in their sights!

On the first Saturday in February, United met QUEENS PARK RANGERS in a Premiership clash at Loftus Road. The first goal came on 18 minutes, from a move instigated by a brilliant throw out by Peter Schmeichel and finished off by Andrei Kanchelskis. Clive Wilson equalised for Rangers on 44 minutes. But before half-time United were back in front through an Eric Cantona header.

Ryan Giggs put United further ahead on the hour, when he made a brilliant run through the Rangers' defence before beating Jan Stejskal. It was a great goal, one of the best yet scored by young Mr Giggs.

Ten minutes later Les Ferdinand pulled one back for Rangers to set up an exciting end to the match. But United held on to take all three points, and chalk up their 20th League victory of the season.

United were next in action in the first leg of the Coca-Cola Cup Semi-Final against SHEFFIELD WEDNESDAY at Old Trafford. In an otherwise evenly-matched contest, Ryan Giggs' quick thinking led to the only goal of the game when he pounced on a woeful defensive error to score in great style.

United's next match was also a Cup tie - this time in the FA Cup Fifth Round, away to WIMBLEDON. The Red Devils dominated the game and hardly allowed the Dons a look-in. A magnificent Eric Cantona volley opened the scoring on 42 minutes. In the second half Paul Ince and Denis Irwin both scored to give United a 3-0 victory and a realtively smooth passage into the Sixth Round.

Six days later it was back to Premiership action

MATCH FAX...FEBRUARY 1994

Premiership			
5.2.94	Loftus Road	Att: 21,267	QPR 2, UNITED 3
26.2.94	Upton Park	Att: 28,382	WEST HAM UNITED 2, UNITED 2
Coca-Cola Cup Semi-Final, First Leg			
13.2.94	Old Trafford	Att: 43,294	UNITED 1, SHEFFIELD WED 0
FA Cup Fifth Round			
20.2.94	Selhurst Park	Att: 27,511	WIMBLEDON 0, UNITED 3

with a visit to WEST HAM UNITED who fought hard to overcome Mark Hughes' 6th minute opener. In fact, with only three minutes left, the Hammers were 2-1 ahead with goals by Lee Chapman and Trevor Morely and it looked as though United were heading for a disastrous defeat.

Then, West Ham old-boy Paul Ince popped up to force the equaliser and save the day.

On 2 March United booked their first Wembley trip of the season by beating SHEFFIELD WEDNESDAY 4-1 at Hillsborough in the Coca-Cola Cup Semi-Final, second leg. United were on top form as they destroyed the Owls with a goal apiece from Brian McClair, Andrei Kanchelskis and two by Mark Hughes. The 5-1 aggregate meant they would meet Aston Villa in the Final.

CHELSEA, the only side to beat United so far in the Premiership campaign, were the visitors to Old Trafford on 5 March. And the Blues became the only team to beat United twice, bringing their 34 match unbeaten run to an end!

The damage was done by Gavin Peacock who scored the only goal of the game, just as he had done in the September fixture. The result meant that Blackburn, who had beaten Liverpool 2-0, edged a little closer to United in the table.

The following Saturday, United were back in FA Cup action, at home to CHARLTON ATHLETIC in the Sixth Round. Just before half-time, with the score at

Cantona outpaces the Sheffield Wednesday defence

0-0, Peter Schmeichel was given his marching orders by referee Robert Hart. The big goalkeeper had handled the ball outside his area - and United were down to ten men.

But the reduction in ranks did little to halt the Red Devils' march to victory. In the opening minute of the second half Mark Hughes broke the deadlock with his second attempt at converting a Ryan Giggs corner. Two goals in four minutes, by Andrei Kanchelskis, put the matter beyond doubt. Charlton's Carl Leaburn pulled one back for the visitors late in the game.

On 16 March United entertained SHEFFIELD WEDNESDAY in the Premiership - and for the fourth time in the season they beat them. This time the scoreline was a resounding 5-0.

By half-time

Above left: Chelsea were the only team to beat United twice in the Premiership in 1993-94

Left: Mark Hughes in action against Swindon

MATCH FAX...MARCH 1994

Coca-Cola Cup Semi-Final, Second Leg			
2.3.94	Hillsborough	Att: 34,878	SHEFFIELD WED 1, UNITED 4
Coca-Cola Cup Final			
27.3.94	Wembley	Att: 77,231	ASTON VILLA 3, UNITED 1
Premiership			
5.3.94	Old Trafford	Att: 44,745	UNITED 0, CHELSEA 1
16.3.94	Old Trafford	Att: 43,669	UNITED 5, SHEFFIELD WED 0
19.3.94	County Ground	Att: 18,102	SWINDON TOWN 2, UNITED 2
22.3.94	Highbury	Att: 36,203	ARSENAL 2, UNITED 2
29.3.94	Old Trafford	Att: 44,751	UNITED 1, LIVERPOOL 0
FA Cup Sixth Round			
12.3.94	Old Trafford	Att: 44,347	UNITED 3, CHARLTON ATH 1

Left: Lee Sharpe celebrates his goal against Arsenal

magnificent Manchester United were four-up. The first came on 18 minutes, after Eric Cantona had delivered an inch-perfect pass over half the length of the pitch to present Ryan Giggs with a scoring chance. Not to be outdone, Mark Hughes produced a piece of magic all of his own two minutes later to score from 35-yards out. Five minutes after that, Paul Ince got his name on the scoresheet with a turn and shot from the edge of the area. Just before half-time Eric Cantona hit the fourth after a brilliant pass from Ince.

Cantona rounded things off very nicely in the 55th minute with his second goal of the game, underlining his Man-of-the-Match status. United looked every inch the Champions elect.

Next came an unexpected 2-2 draw with SWINDON TOWN at The County Ground on 19 March. The two clubs, representing both ends of the Premiership table, played out a fascinating drama which twice saw United's lead snatched from them. Roy Keane (13 mins) and Paul Ince (62 mins) scored for United, Luc Nijholt (36 mins) and Jan Fjortoft (83 mins) for Swindon. Eric Cantona was sent-off for 'violent conduct' in the 66th minute.

Another 2-2 draw followed on 22 March, this time against ARSENAL at Highbury. Lee Sharpe opened United's account on 10 minutes when he pounced on a mistake by David Seaman. But that lead was wiped out 26 minutes later when Gary Pallister deflected the ball into his own net from an Arsenal free-kick.

Sharpe put United back into the lead during another penalty-area scramble in the 53rd minute, but Paul Merson restored the Gunners' pride after another set piece situation in the 78th minute.

That took care of all the goals, but there was more drama to come when Eric Cantona collected his second booking of the game and received his second red card in four days.

On 27 March United made their first Wembley appearance of 1994 - in the Coca-Cola Cup Final against ASTON VILLA. There was much talk of United winning the 'treble' of Premiership, League Cup and FA Cup triumphs. Indeed, that feat was in their sights. But Villa boss Ron Atkinson, a former Manchester United manager, had the measure of his old club - just as he had with Sheffield Wednesday in the Final of the same competition in 1991. On the day, Villa took United apart to win 3-1 with a goal from Dalian Atkinson and two from Dean Saunders. Mark Hughes scored for United.

Disappointed though they were, the team was back in the thick of the

Paul Ince heads the winner in the home match against Liverpool

Left: 'Who's a cheeky boy then!' Paul Ince gets to grips with Blackburn's Alan Shearer

Premiership action three days later with the visit of LIVERPOOL to Old Trafford. After all, the 'double' was still a possibility!

The game, played out in front of the biggest Premiership crowd of the season so far, was settled by a single goal, headed home by Paul Ince in the 37th minute, from a Lee Sharpe corner.

United were back on track and had stretched ahead of Blackburn Rovers, the team they were due to meet in the very next fixture.

BLACKBURN ROVERS narrowed the gap between themselves and United on 2 April, with a solid 2-0 victory at Ewood Park. The brilliant Alan Shearer did the damage with two classic strikes on 46 and 76 minutes.

United, weakened by the discipline-enforced absence of Eric Cantona, looked somewhat jaded and could find no answer to the problems posed by Kenny Dalglish's side. But they were still three points ahead at the top of the table.

OLDHAM ATHLETIC came to Old Trafford on 4 April in the Premiership, knowing they were to meet United six days later in the Semi-Final of the FA Cup at Wembley.

Both clubs needed the points - United to keep ahead in the title race, Athletic to keep out of the relegation danger-zone. It was a close-run thing, but United emerged as 3-2 victors with goals from Ryan Giggs, Dion Dublin and Paul Ince.

The two teams met again at Wembley on 10 April to play for a place in the FA Cup Final against Chelsea, who had defeated plucky Luton Town in the other Wembley Semi-Final 24 hours earlier.

After 90 minutes there was still no score and the game went into extra time. Then, after 106 minutes of gruelling effort by both sides, OLDHAM went ahead through Neil Pointon and continued to hold out. Right up to the last minute, the Latics must have thought they'd done enough.

But they reckoned without Mark Hughes who, in the dying seconds of the game, forced his way between two defenders to

Left: United's flying winger Andrei Kanchelskis in Semi-Final action against Oldham

Ryan Giggs slips past Oldham's Neil Pointon

thump a tremendous volley into the back of Jon Hallworth's net. United's players and fans alike all breathed a sigh of relief and looked forward to a hard-earned replay, - the third consecutive match between the two clubs - which took place three days later at Manchester City's Maine Road ground.

This time United made no mistake. Within 15 minutes they were two-up through Denis Irwin and Andrei Kanchelskis. Neil Pointon pulled one back for OLDHAM on 39 minutes. But Bryan Robson and Ryan Giggs added two more in the second half to make the final scoreline 4-1. United were in their 12th FA Cup Final.

So, with the 'double' still looking a distinct possibility United travelled to Selhurst Park for the League clash with WIMBLEDON on 16 April. Their ambitions suffered quite a jolt as the Dons beat them 1-0, with a John Fashanu goal. United were again without the suspended Eric Cantona - and they definitely missed him!

But the mercurial French star - the PFA's Player of the Year - was back in action in United's next match, at home to neighbours MANCHESTER CITY, and he stamped his authority all over the place by scoring both goals in a 2-0 victory. United were back on track.

On 27 April United chalked up a convincing 2-0 away win over LEEDS UNITED, with goals by Andrei Kanchelskis and Ryan Giggs - both of them created by Mark Hughes.

On May Day, United went to Portman Road to take on IPSWICH TOWN. It was a tough match with Ipswich fighting for Premiership survival. The home side opened the scoring with a Chris Kiwomya goal on 19 minutes, but ultimately United proved the superior force and goals from Eric Cantona

Below: What a relief! Mark Hughes has just scored that last minute equaliser against Oldham in the FA Cup Semi-Final

Ryan Giggs and Rick Holden race for the ball in the Wembley Semi-Final

and Ryan Giggs secured the three points.

The next day Blackburn finally fell out of the title race with a 2-1 defeat at the hands of Coventry.

United were Champions again! They celebrated with yet another win on 4 May, 2-0 at home to SOUTHAMPTON, in front of 44,705 ecstatic fans. The goals came from Andrei Kanchelskis and Mark Hughes.

COVENTRY CITY, who had helped secure the title for United, were Old Trafford's last Premiership visitors of the season on 8 May. A 0-0 draw did nothing to spoil the party atmosphere.

United had won the Premiership with 92 points, the record since the introduction of the 3 points for a win system.

After the game, Steve Bruce stepped up to receive the Premiership trophy - and he invited Bryan Robson to join him. It was a

United's penalty-king Eric Cantona

fine gesture which underlined the team spirit that permeates Old Trafford these days!

Now all that remained in United's quest for the elusive 'double' was the Final against Chelsea, winners in both of the season's previous fixtures between the two clubs.

The FA Cup Final was played on 14 May in driving rain. In the first half, United were definitely below par. CHELSEA were in charge and went closest to scoring, but Gavin Peacock's dipping shot from 20 yards rebounded off Peter Schmeichel's crossbar.

"In the second half, we played like Manchester United," said Alex Ferguson after the event. Indeed, it looked like a different United who strode out onto Wembley's wet turf and eventually took the game by the scruff of its neck.

It was a tale of two penalites that finally broke Chelsea's resolve. The first came on the hour, after Eddie Newton had sent Denis Irwin flying on the edge of the box. The spot kick was nonchalantly converted by Eric Cantona as Dimitri Kharin dived the wrong way.

The second penalty, five minutes later, was a more controversial affair. United fans would say that Frank Sinclair illegally bundled Andrei Kanchelskis off the ball just inside the box. The Chelsea camp would argue that Sinclair made a perfectly legal shoulder charge just outside the area.

Referee David Elleray, the man whose opinion mattered most, instantly pointed to the spot. Again Eric Cantona took the kick and again Kharin went the wrong way. United were two-up.

Chelsea boss Glenn

Denis Irwin opens the scoring against Oldham in the Semi-Final Replay at Maine road

United players celebrate their finest ever season

United at 'the double'

Hoddle brought himself into the fray as the battling Blues desperately attempted to gain lost ground. But, on 69 minutes, a defensive error let in Mark Hughes to add a third and put the game beyond the Londoners' reach.

The game had been turned on its head in nine dramatic minutes. But still there was more to come. In the last minute substitute Brian McClair rounded off the scoreline at 4-0 with a simple tap-in from a pass unselfishly supplied by Paul Ince.

Manchester United had become only the sixth team in English football history to 'do the double'.

Now Alex Ferguson and his side are seeking to improve on their recently created legend - by lifting the European Cup...

MATCH FAX...APRIL/MAY 1994

Premiership			
1.4.94	Ewood Park	Att: 20,866	BLACKBURN ROVERS 2, UNITED 0
4.4.94	Old Trafford	Att: 44,686	UNITED 3, OLDHAM ATHLETIC 2
16.4.94	Selhurst Park	Att: 28,553	WIMBLEDON 1, UNITED 0
23.4.94	Old Trafford	Att: 44,333	UNITED 2, MANCHESTER CITY 0
27.4.94	Elland Road	Att: 41,125	LEEDS UNITED 0, UNITED 2
1.5.94	Portman Road	Att: 22,559	IPSWICH TOWN 1, UNITED 2
8.5.94	Old Trafford	Att: 44,717	UNITED 0, COVENTRY CITY 0
FA Cup Semi-Final			
10.4.94	Wembley	Att: 56,399	UNITED 1, OLDHAM ATHLETIC 1
FA Cup Semi-Final Replay			
13.4.94	Maine Road	Att: 32,211	UNITED 4, OLDHAM ATHLETIC 1
FA Cup Final			
14.5.95	Wembley	Att: 79,634	CHELSEA 0, UNITED 4

MANCHESTER UNITED'S

ROLL OF HONOUR

COMPETITION	No. TIMES	DATES
LEAGUE CHAMPIONS	7	1907-08, 1910-11, 1951-52, 1955-56, 1956-57, 1964-65,1966-67
PREMIER LEAGUE CHAMPIONS	2	1992-93, 1993-94
CHAMPIONSHIP RUNNERS-UP	10	1946-47, 1947-48, 1948-49, 1950-51, 1958-59, 1963-64, 1967-68, 1979-80, 1987-88, 1991-92
SECOND DIVISION CHAMPIONS	2	1935-36, 1974-75
SECOND DIVISION RUNNERS-UP	4	1896-97, 1905-06, 1924-25, 1937-38
FA CUP WINNERS	8	1909, 1948, 1963, 1977, 1983, 1985, 1990, 1994
FA CUP RUNNERS-UP	4	1957, 1958, 1976, 1979
LEAGUE CUP WINNERS	1	1992
LEAGUE CUP RUNNERS-UP	3	1983, 1991, 1994
EUROPEAN CUP WINNERS	1	1968
EUROPEAN CUP-WINNERS' CUP WINNERS	1	1991